THE STORY OF MY LIFE

THE STORY OF MY LIFE

Helen Keller

Om KIDZ
An imprint of Om Books International

First published in 2020

Om KIDZ | Om Books International

Corporate & Editorial Office
A-12, Sector 64, Noida 201 301
Uttar Pradesh, India
Phone: +91 120 477 4100
Email: editorial@ombooks.com
Website: www.ombooksinternational.com

Sales Office
107, Ansari Road, Darya Ganj,
New Delhi 110 002, India
Phone: +91 11 4000 9000
Email: sales@ombooks.com

Retold by Swayam Ganguly

ISBN: 978-93-5376-430-2

Printed in India

10 9 8 7 6 5 4 3 2 1

Contents

1. The Strange Illness 7
2. My Best Friends 21
3. A Lengthy Trip 33
4. Miss Sullivan Arrives 41
5. The Tree of Paradise 51
6. Comprehension of Love 59
7. Helen Learns to Read 69
8. Christmas 85
9. Travelling to Boston 91
10. The Ocean and the Woods 101
11. Stormy Days 119
12. Learning to Speak 125
13. The Frost King 137
14. Preparing for College 155
15. Wright-Humason 169
16. Cambridge 177
17. Gilman School 193
18. Radcliffe 207
19. A Love Affair with Literature 215
20. Other Pleasures 223
21. Acknowledgements 229

About the Author 236

Characters 237

Questions 238

Chapter One

The Strange Illness

A strange fear grips me as I begin to pen down the history of my life. A superstitious hesitation exists when I try to lift the veil that obscures my childhood like a golden mist. Writing an autobiography is one of the most difficult tasks, and when I attempt to chronicle my earliest impressions, I discover that fact and fantasy appear the same in the years that link the past with the present. The woman paints the child's experiences in her own fantasy. Some impressions are vividly striking from the early years of my life, although the shadows of the prison-house weigh heavily on the rest. Also,

many of the happiness and sorrows of my childhood have lost their pathos; and numerous important, vital incidents during my early years have been relegated to the dark recesses of the mind, thanks to the excitement of great discoveries. Therefore, I shall provide a series of sketches that cover only the important and most interesting episodes of my life.

I was born in Tuscumbia, a small town in northern Alabama, on 27 June 1880. My father's family had descended from Caspar Keller, a native of Switzerland, who decided to settle in Maryland. One of our Swiss ancestors was the first teacher of the deaf in Zurich. He also authored a book on how to educate them. Caspar Keller's son, my grandfather, occupied large tracts of land in Alabama, finally settling there. I've heard that he travelled once a year on horseback from Tuscumbia to Philadelphia to procure supplies the plantation needed. My aunt is in possession of the letters he wrote to his family, that give fascinating and vivid

accounts of these trips. Grandmother Keller was the granddaughter of an early colonial governor of Virginia named Alexander Spotswood, and the second cousin to Robert E. Lee. My father, Arthur H. Keller, was a captain in the Confederate Army. My mother, Kate Adams, was his second wife and considerably younger than him. Benjamin Adams, her grandfather, married Susana E. Goodhue, and resided in Newbury, Massachusetts, for several years. Their son was named Charles Adams, and he moved to Helena, Arkansas. After the outbreak of the Civil War, he fought on the side of the South, and was promoted to the rank of Brigadier-General. He married Lucy Helen Everett, who belonged to the same illustrious family of Everetts as Edward Everett and Dr Edward Everett Hale. The family moved to Memphis, Tennessee, after the war was over.

When I was afflicted by the illness that deprived me of my sight and hearing, I lived in a small house comprising a large square room and a tiny room, that served as the servants'

quarters. It is customary in the South to build a small house near the homestead to be used occasionally. My father constructed a similar house after the Civil War and lived in it with my mother after their marriage. This house was covered with vines, climbing roses and honeysuckles, resembling an arbour when viewed from the garden. The small porch was obscured by a screen of yellow roses and southern smilax. Hummingbirds and bees loved visiting this place. The Keller homestead, where the family resided, was a few steps away from our little rose-bower that was christened 'Ivy Green', because beautiful English ivy decorated the house, the fences and the surrounding trees. Its old-fashioned garden was simply paradise on earth!

Much before my teacher arrived in my life, guided by the sense of smell, I would discover the first lilies and violets. After a sudden fit of temper, I would head there to find solace, and would hide my hot face in the cool grass

and leaves. It was such joy to lose myself in that flower garden, happily wandering from spot to spot, till I suddenly arrived upon a beautiful vine, recognisable by its leaves and blossoms. It instantly dawned upon me that it was the vine that covered the tumble-down summer-house at the back end of the garden. Here, as well, were trailing clematis, drooping jessamine, and rare sweet flowers named butterfly lilies. They owed their name thanks to their fragile petals, resembling the wings of butterflies. The roses were the loveliest of them all! The greenhouses of the North could not have boasted of a lovelier collection like the climbing roses of my Southern home. They hung resplendently in long festoons from our porch, enveloping the entire air with their fragrance, undisturbed by any other earthly smell. At dawn, soaked in the dew, they emanated a softness and purity that resembled the asphodels of God's own garden.

My early life was rather simple. Just like any other first baby in the family, I came, I saw, and I conquered. The normal amount of discussion took place as to what should be a proper name for me. It was improper for the first baby of the family to be lightly named, and everyone was firm about that. The name 'Mildred Campbell' was suggested by my father, for an ancestor he highly revered. My mother solved the problem by insisting that I should be named after her mother, whose maiden name was Helen Everett. But, in the sheer excitement of carrying me to church, my father lost the name on the way. This was natural as it was not his preferred name after all. When the minister asked for my name, he just recalled that it had been decided that I be named after my grandmother. So, he gave the name as Helen Adams. I have been informed that I was a good mimic in my early years. I could say, "How d'ye" at six months, and one day, I was the cynosure of all eyes by saying "tea, tea, tea".

Even post my illness I remembered one word that I had learned quite early. The word was 'water'. I walked as soon as I turned one year old. But those happy days didn't last long! The dreary month of February brought the illness that closed my ears and eyes and flung me into the unconsciousness of a newly born. It was termed as the acute congestion of the stomach and brain, and the doctor stated that I wouldn't survive!

But one morning, the fever disappeared as mysteriously as it had arrived. Everyone in the family rejoiced, but none of them had any idea, not even the doctor, that I would not see or hear again. I still have confused memories of that illness. What I remember clearly is the tenderness with which my mother used to soothe me when I was wailing in fear and pain. Slowly, I got accustomed to the silence and darkness that surrounded me and came to terms with the fact that it had been different once. Then, she arrived – my teacher, and she set my spirit free! During the first 19 months of my life, I had seen broad, green fields, a luminous sky, and trees and flowers which this present darkness could not blot out entirely.

Chapter Two

My Best Friends

I do not remember exactly what happened in the first months after my illness struck. I just recall sitting on my mother's lap and clutching her dress as she went about her domestic chores. My hands felt every object and motion, and I discovered many things in this way. Soon, I started making crude signs as I was desirous of communication with others. A shake of the head denoted "no" and a nod meant "yes". A pull signified "come" and a push meant "go".

If I wanted bread, I would mimic the act of cutting the slices and buttering them. If I longed for ice cream, I would make the sign for

working the freezer, and shiver, to denote cold. Thanks to my mother, I was able to understand a great deal, and I owe everything to her loving wisdom.

When I was five years old, I learned to fold and put away the clean clothes when they arrived from the laundry. I also knew how to separate my own clothes from the rest. I could gauge by the way my mother and aunt dressed that they were going out and begged them to take me along. I knew by sounds when guests arrived in the house and learned how to dress on my own to join their company. But it was frustrating that my mother and friends did not use signs as I did when they wanted things done. They spoke with their mouths and this made me very angry.

A little girl named Martha Washington, who was the child of our cook, and an old dog named Belle, a great hunter in her younger days, were my good friends. Martha Washington comprehended my signs and was submissive to my commands. I loved dominating her, and always had my way, even if it meant fighting tooth and nail for it. We spent a lot of time in the kitchen together, doing things like kneading dough balls and feeding the hens and turkeys that gathered about the kitchen steps. They were so tame that they fed off our hands and let us feel them. Once, a big turkey stole a tomato from my hand and ran off with it.

I loved looking for guinea-fowl eggs in the long grass. I never allowed Martha to carry the eggs home when we discovered them, as she might have fallen and broken them. Martha and I were greatly interested in the corn sheds, horse stables, and the yards where the cows were milked. The milkers permitted me to keep my hands on the cows while they were milked, and my inquisitiveness often led to the cow switching me.

Getting ready for Christmas was delightful. I had no idea what it signified then, but the pleasant odours in the house were heavenly. We were allowed to grind the spices, pick over the raisins, and lick the stirring spoons. I hung my stockings because I was supposed to, but it was not something that was particularly interesting. Neither was I excited to wake up early to see what gifts I had received.

Martha Washington was two or three years older than me but was as fond of mischief as I was. One day, we were cutting paper dolls together, but were soon bored. We cut off our shoelaces and all the leaves off the honeysuckle within reach for further amusement. Martha had little bunches of fuzzy hair tied with shoestrings. These stuck out all over her head like corkscrews. I started cutting off her corkscrews, and insisting on fair play, she cut off one of my curls. But for the timely intervention of my mother, we would have cut off each other's hair completely.

Belle, the old dog, my other friend, was a lazy creature. She preferred a siesta by the fire

rather than romping with me. She displayed no interest in learning the sign language I tried to teach her. Many incidents from my childhood are etched in my memory; isolated, intense, yet full of clarity. I spilled water on my apron once and spread it out to dry before the fire on the sitting-room hearth. It did not dry as quickly as I wanted, and I drew closer to the fire and flung it on the hot ashes. The fire jumped to life, and the flames enveloped me! As my clothes blazed, my terrified scream brought Viny, my old nurse, to the rescue. She almost suffocated me by throwing a blanket over me. But she put out the fire. I just received minor burns on my hands and hair.

During this time, I discovered the use of a key. One morning, I locked my mother in the pantry for three hours. As she pounded on the door, I laughed with glee. This naughty prank convinced my parents that a teacher must be obtained for me. After my teacher, Miss Sullivan arrived, I waited for a chance to lock her up in

her room. I managed to do that, and my father had to get a ladder and get Miss Sullivan out through the window, much to my delight.

When I was five years old, we moved to a bigger house. Our family was made up of my parents, two older half-brothers, and later, a younger sister named Mildred. My earliest memory of my father was to make my way through great drifts of newspapers to find him holding a sheet of paper before his face. It was greatly puzzling then, and it was only later that I realised what those papers were, and that my father edited one of them. He was a loving father, who rarely left home, except for the hunting season. He was a great hunter and an expert marksman. After his family, he loved his dog and gun the most. He loved hosting people, and the big garden where he grew the best strawberries and watermelons in the country, was his pride. For me, he brought home the first ripe grapes and the best berries.

It was the summer of 1896. I was enjoying my holiday in the North, when I received news of my father's death. He had been afflicted with a brief illness and had suffered acutely. That was my first great sorrow, and my first brush with death.

I loved my mother so much that I was intensely jealous of my sister. I perceived her to be an intruder and was angry when my mother used to devote so much time to the baby. One day, I discovered Mildred sleeping peacefully in my favourite doll Nancy's cradle. In a rush of blood to my head, I overturned the cradle. The baby would have been killed if my mother hadn't caught her. But later, when human qualities were embedded in me, Mildred and I grew to love each other, and became inseparable. We walked hand in hand, even though she did not comprehend my sign language, nor I her childish prattle.

Chapter Three

A Lengthy Trip

The desire to express myself grew steadily. The signs I made were not enough, and frustration set in when I failed to make myself understood. I broke down in tears and exhaustion, seeking solace in my mother's arms. These passionate outbursts took place daily, sometimes hourly. My parents were saddened and perplexed. We resided a long way from the school for the deaf or the blind, and it was inconceivable that a teacher would come to a far-flung place like Tuscumbia to teach me. My relatives and friends also doubted if I was capable of learning. Charles

Dickens was the only one who inspired hope in my mother. She had read his account of Laura Bridgman in his 'American Notes', and recalled that she was deaf and blind, yet received an education. But she also recalled that Dr Howe, the man credited with discovering the way to teach the deaf and the blind, had died many years ago. But had his methods died with him as well? Even if they hadn't, how was it possible for a little girl in a remote town in Alabama to avail them?

I was six years old when my father received news about an eminent oculist in Baltimore. He was supposedly a miracle worker, and my parents resolved to take me to Baltimore to see if my eyes could be treated. This journey was pleasant, and I made many friends on the train. A lady gifted me a box of shells, in which my father made holes so that I could string them. This kept me happily engaged for a long time. The nice conductor

let me cling on to his coat-tails while he went around collecting and punching tickets. He also let me play with his punch. It was a lovely toy with which I punched funny little holes in bits of cardboard. My aunt created a big doll out of towels for me. Strangely, it had no nose, mouth, ears or eyes. But the absence of the eyes struck me the most out of all the other defects. I pointed this out to everybody, but no one seemed capable of providing the doll with eyes. Suddenly, an idea struck me, and the problem was resolved. I looked for my aunt's cape, which was trimmed with large beads. Pulling two beads off, I communicated to her that they be sewn on my doll. After this was achieved, my joy knew no bounds! But then, I lost interest in the doll. Dr Chisholm received us warmly in Baltimore, but regretted after inspecting me that he could do nothing. He stated that I could be educated, and referred me to Dr Alexander Graham Bell of Washington. He would be able to provide information on schools and teachers for deaf and blind children, he said. We arrived in Washington and met Dr Bell. I felt the warmth and kindness of Dr Bell that had endeared him to so many hearts, just as his wonderful achievements had made him famous. I inspected his watch as he held me on his knee. He made me strike it. I loved him as he understood all my signs, but I had no clue that this was the interview that would help me walk through the door of darkness into the light, and from seclusion to knowledge! My father was advised by Dr Bell to write to Mr Anagnos, director of the Perkins Institute in Boston. This is where Dr Howe had laboured extensively for the blind, and this is where a teacher could be found for me. My father did so and received a reply after a few weeks in the form of a kind letter, that informed him that a teacher had been found. It was the summer of 1886, but Miss Sullivan arrived only the following March. This is how I emerged from Egypt and stood before Sinai. A divine power blessed me with magical vision to witness the wonders of the world. I heard a voice from the sacred mountain, that proclaimed, "Knowledge is love and light and vision."

Chapter Four

Miss Sullivan arrives

The day my teacher, Anne Mansfield Sullivan arrived was the most important day in my life. The date was 3 March 1887, just three months before I turned seven. That afternoon, I stood on the perch, confused yet expectant. From the rush and the signs that my mother made, I guessed that something significant was about to occur. I was unaware of what the future had in store for me and was experiencing constant bouts of anger and bitterness.

Have you ever been at sea, imprisoned by a dense fog? It is like being obscured by a tangible white darkness as the huge ship manoeuvres its

way slowly and cautiously towards the safety of the shore with plummet and sounding line. Your heart beats like a thousand drums as you wait for something to happen! I was just like that ship on that eventful day. The only difference was that I lacked a compass or sounding-line and had no clue how distant the harbour was. "Light! Give me light!" my soul cried wordlessly, and that very instant, the light of love shone on me. I heard approaching footsteps, and extended my hand, thinking it was my mother. Someone took my hand, and I was held close in her arms. It was she! She had arrived to reveal the light of knowledge to me, and more importantly, to love me!

My teacher, Miss Sullivan, led me to her room and gifted me a doll sent by the little blind children at the Perkins Institution. I learnt only later that Laura Bridgman had dressed it. After I had played with my doll for a while, Miss Sullivan slowly spelled the word 'd-o-l-l' into my hand. I was instantly interested in this finger

play and tried imitating it. I felt great pleasure and pride when I succeeded, and ran upstairs to my mother. I demonstrated my new skill without the knowledge that words existed or that I was spelling a word. My fingers were just involved in monkey-like imitation. In the days that followed, I learned to spell many words in this manner like 'cup', 'hat pin', and a few verbs like 'sit', 'stand' and 'walk'. But it was only after spending many weeks with my teacher before I comprehended that everything had a name.

One day, Miss Sullivan put my big rag doll into my lap as I was playing with it. Spelling 'd-o-l-l', she tried to make me understand that 'd-o-l-l' applied to the doll. In the earlier part of the day, we had had a tussle over the words 'w-a-t-e-r' and 'm-u-g.'

She had tried her best to teach me that the two were separate words. But I failed to understand, and she had dropped the topic in despair only to renew it again whenever the opportunity presented itself. Her repeated

attempts irritated me, and I grabbed the new doll to dash it upon the floor. The broken fragments of the doll delighted me, and I experienced neither sadness nor regret at my action. Sentiments like love and tenderness did not exist in the dark world I resided in.

I heard my teacher sweep away the broken fragments and felt satisfied that the cause of my discomfort was removed. She fetched my hat, and I was joyous that we would be going out in the warm sunshine. I hopped and skipped in joy as we walked down to the well-house. The smell of the honeysuckle that covered it attracted me like a bee to honey. Suddenly, my teacher placed my hand under the spout where someone was drawing water. As the cool stream flowed over my hand, Miss Sullivan spelled the word 'water' over the other hand, first slowly, and then rapidly.

I was transfixed, my entire attention focused on her finger movements. Suddenly, I experienced a foggy consciousness of something forgotten, and a strange thrill of sudden recall. In a rush of déjà vu, the mystery of language was revealed as it dawned on me that the cool and wonderful thing overflowing on my hand was 'w-a-t-e-r'. That living word liberated my senses and awakened my soul. It gave it light, hope and happiness, setting it completely free.

I left the well-house with an eagerness to learn more! Now I knew that everything had a name. I saw everything with the strange new vision I had been suddenly blessed with. I recalled the doll I had broken and went to the corner of the hearth where the pieces lay. In vain, I tried to put the pieces together again. Then, after realising that this was impossible and what I had done, my eyes welled up in tears. For the first time, I experienced feelings of repentance and sorrow.

I do not remember all the words I learned that day, but I do remember that they were numerous. 'Father', 'mother', 'sister' and 'teacher' are the few I recall. These words would make my world blossom, and I was one of the happiest children that day with my new-found knowledge. That night, for the first time in my life, I longed for a new day to dawn.

Chapter Five

The Tree of Paradise

I can recollect numerous incidents from the summer of 1887 that preceded the sudden liberation of my soul. When daisies and buttercups bloomed, Miss Sullivan led me by the hand across the fields to the banks of the Tennessee River. There, seated on the warm grass, I learned how the rain and the sun are responsible for the growth of trees and food, how birds built their nests, and how animals found food and shelter. As my knowledge expanded, so did my happiness in being a part of this world. Much before I mastered arithmetic or geography, Miss Sullivan taught me to bask

in the beauty of every single blade of grass in the fragrant woods. I also learned to find joy in the curves and dimples of my baby sister's hand. Miss Sullivan merged my earliest thoughts with nature, and I became best friends with the birds and flowers.

But I also learned that nature can be cruel sometimes. My teacher and I were returning from a long walk one day. We had rested a couple of times, and our last halt was under a wild cherry tree, a short distance from home. It was an easy tree to climb, and we found a seat in the branches. Miss Sullivan proposed that we have our lunch here, and I promised to sit still while she went home to fetch it.

Suddenly, I felt a change come over the tree as the warmth of the sun vanished. I realised the sky was black now as the heat had faded away from the atmosphere, and because this very heat was light to me. The earth radiated a strange odour that preceded a thunderstorm. My heart was thumping with a strange fear. This was the

fear of the unknown and I was struck numb. I wished desperately that my teacher would return, but wished the most to get off that tree.

The silence was sinister, and the continuous swaying of the leaves added to the terror. The wind howled with such fury that I was almost swept off the tree. I managed to cling on for dear life to the branch as the tree swayed threateningly. The small twigs snapped and fell about me in small showers. I was seized with a wild impulse to jump, but my fear restrained me. The branches lashed at me, and just when I thought that the tree would crash to the earth my teacher caught my hands and helped me down. I clung to her bosom; I had learnt a new lesson - that nature does not shy away from waging open war against her children, and that under the softest touch, treacherous claws lie concealed.

I did not dare climb a tree till a long time. The sweet enticement of the mimosa tree in full bloom finally aided me to overcome this fear.

On a beautiful spring morning, I was alone in the summer-house when a subtle fragrance in the air arrested my senses. It was as if the spirit of spring had invaded the summer-house. I recognised the odour of the mimosa blossoms. I reached the mimosa tree and touched it. It was quivering in the warm sunshine, and the blossom-laden branches were almost kissing the long grass. I pulled myself up the tree by placing my foot in the wide space between the forked branches. I experienced some difficulty hanging on, as the branches were huge and the bark hurt my little hands. But the realisation of doing something wonderful egged me on, and I climbed higher and higher to reach a small seat someone had built so long ago that it was almost like a part of the tree now. I sat there for a long time, just like a fairy on a rosy cloud. After that day, I spent many happy hours in my tree of paradise, dreaming bright dreams and thinking beautiful thoughts.

Chapter Six

Comprehension of Love

The key to language was now at my disposal, and I was eager to use it. Children capable of hearing can do this with nominal effort, catching the words emitted from the lips of others easily. But a deaf child must trap these words in a slow and painful process. But the end-result is wonderful irrespective of the process.

Slowly after naming an object, we progress step by step until we have covered the considerable distance between our first stuttered syllable to the language of Shakespeare. Initially, when my teacher introduced me to a new thing, I asked a few questions. The ability to grasp

was weak and my vocabulary was inadequate. But as my knowledge expanded, and I picked up more and more words, my inquisitiveness increased. I would return to the same subject repeatedly, hungry for more information. Sometimes, a new word revived an image that had existed in my brain thanks to some prior experience.

I recall the morning I enquired what the word 'love' meant. This was before I had picked up many words. I had discovered a few violets in the garden, picked them, and brought them to Miss Sullivan. She had tried to kiss me, but at that time, I did not like to be kissed by anyone except my mother. So, Miss Sullivan gently put her hand around me, and spelled into my hand, 'I love Helen.'

"What is love?" I asked.

"It is here," she said, pointing to her heart as she drew me closer. I was conscious of a heartbeat for the very first time. Her words were confusing then as I did not comprehend anything

unless I touched it. I smelled the violets and then asked a question half in signs and half in words, that went, "Is love the sweetness of flowers?"

"No," Miss Sullivan replied.

"Is this love?" I asked, pointing at the direction of the sun from where the heat descended upon us. I was convinced that the sun was the most beautiful thing on earth as its heat made things grow. I was naturally disappointed and confused when Miss Sullivan shook her head in the negative. It was strange, I thought, that my teacher was unable to show me what 'love' was. A couple of days later, I was busy stringing beads of various sizes in symmetrical groups. There were two large beads, three small ones, and so on. I had made many mistakes, and my teacher had pointed them out with great patience and perseverance repeatedly. Finally, I noticed a rather obvious mistake in the sequence and focused on the lesson with great concentration. "Think," Miss Sullivan touched

my head, and spelled with great emphasis.

In a flash, I was aware that the word was the name of the process that was taking place in my head. This was the first time I had consciously perceived an abstract idea. I was still for a long time, not thinking of the beads that lay on my lap but trying to discover the meaning of 'love' in lieu of this new idea. The sun had been obscured by clouds all day, and there had been some intermittent showers. Then, the sun shone in its resplendent southern splendour suddenly.

"Is this not love?" I asked Miss Sullivan.

"Love is something like the clouds that existed in the sky before the sun came out," she replied. Then, she explained in simpler words, "Unlike the rain which you can feel, the clouds cannot be touched. You realise how happy the flowers and the earth are to quench their thirst after a hot day because of the rain. Just like the clouds, you cannot touch love either, but the sweetness that it shares with everything can be felt. Without love, you would not be happy!"

The beautiful truth dawned on me at last! I realised that there were invisible lines that existed between my and the spirits of others, thereby connecting them. Ever since Miss Sullivan had started educating me, she had ensured that she spoke to me just as she spoke to any other child. The noticeable difference was that she spelled the words into my hand instead of speaking them. As the deaf child does not learn in a month, or a couple of years, this process continued for many years.

The small hearing child picks up these idioms and expressions thanks to constant imitation and repetition. The conversation he hears in his house stimulates his mind and gives release to his own freedom of expression of thought. But the deaf child is denied of this natural exchange of ideas. My teacher was aware of the problem, and hence, she left no stone unturned to provide me with the stimulus I needed. But it was a long time before I showed the inclination to take part in a conversation despite all her efforts. I even took longer to say something right at the right time.

It is indeed difficult for the deaf and blind to pick up the art of conversation. It is difficult for them to distinguish the tone of voice or recognise tones that form words without proper guidance. They are without the advantage of watching the expressions on the speaker's face, and as they say, a look is often the very soul of speech!

Chapter Seven

Helen Learns to Read

The next important step in my education process was learning to read. Miss Sullivan gave me slips of cardboard as soon as I could spell a few words. These slips of cardboard had printed words in raised letters on them, and I quickly grasped that each printed word represented an object, act or quality. I was given a frame in which I could arrange the words in small sentences; but even before I arranged the sentences in the frame, I used to make them in objects. Taking the slips of paper that represented things like 'bed', 'doll', 'on', and 'is', I placed them on the objects themselves. Then, I placed the doll on

the bed with the word 'is' and 'on' thus making a sentence. But I also executed the act that the sentence represented.

I pinned the word 'girl' on my pinafore and stood in the wardrobe. I arranged the words 'is' and 'in' and 'wardrobe' on the shelf. This game delighted me the most, and Miss Sullivan and I played it for hours on end. The room was often arranged in object sentences by us. It was a natural progression from the printed slip to the printed book. I hunted for familiar words in 'Reader for Beginners', and my joy knew no bounds when I discovered them. This is how I began reading. I received no regular lessons for a long time, and even when I studied most seriously, it was more play than work. Miss Sullivan taught everything to me through a beautiful poem or story. If anything arrested my interest, she discussed it as if she were a small child herself. What most children dread is the painful plodding through grammar, difficult math, and tougher definitions. Those are my most precious memories today.

Maybe Miss Sullivan had a natural affinity towards me, or her expertise was because of her lengthy association with the blind. But the dedication to her work was unquestionable. She had an exceptional eye for detail, and never nagged me for answers. She introduced the intricacies of science to me slowly, ensuring that the teaching was so real that I remembered everything she taught me.

We studied outdoors, preferring the warmth of the woods to indoor study. The smell of the woods is engraved in my early lessons - that sublime odour of pine needles blended with wild grapes. Anything that bloomed, hummed, buzzed or sang was instrumental in furthering my education like crickets, noisy-throated frogs, chickens, wildflowers, dogwood blossoms, meadow-violets, and budding fruit trees. I found delight in feeling the softness of the budding cotton balls and in listening to the soft rustle of the leaves as the wind blew right through them. I recall the snort of my pony and

the spicy, clovery smell of his breath.

At dawn sometimes, I crept into the garden which was heavy with the dew resting on the flowers and the grass. What joy it is to feel the roses pressing softly into the hands and the sway of the lilies in the morning breeze! There were times when my fingers would meet an insect in the flower I was plucking. I could feel the pair of wings moving frantically in sudden terror as the little creature became aware of an external presence.

The orchard was another favourite haunt of mine, and the fruit here ripened in early July. The big peaches would be begging to be picked and the breeze would make apples fall at my feet. I would delightedly pick up the apples, feeling the sunny warmth of their freshness against my cheek.

The favourite walk was to Keller's Landing, an old tumbledown lumber-wharf on the Tennessee River. During the Civil War, it was used to land soldiers. We spent many happy hours here and this was our place for geography lessons. I built dams of pebbles, created fictitious islands and lakes, and dug river-beds, having so much fun without ever realising that I was being taught a lesson.

I was spellbound as Miss Sullivan told me stories about the great round world with its buried cities, burning mountains, moving rivers, and other strange things. She created raised maps in clay, so it was easier for me to comprehend and distinguish between mountain ridges and valleys, and so that I could follow the deceptive course of rivers with my fingers. But I found the division of the earth into poles and zones utterly confusing, and even today, the mere mention of the temperate zone indicates a series of twine circles to me.

Arithmetic was the only part of my education I had an aversion to. My teacher attempted making me count by stringing beads in groups. I learned to add and subtract by the arrangement of kindergarten straws. But I always lacked the patience to arrange more than five or six groups at one time. I studied botany and zoology in the same lazy manner.

Once a gentleman, whose name I forget, sent me a collection of fossils. These were tiny mollusc shells that were beautifully marked, sandstone parts with bird claw prints, and a beautiful bas-relief fern. These gifts opened the antediluvian world for me, and I heard Miss Sullivan describe the terrible beasts who had uncouth, unpronounceable names. They stormed through the primeval forests, smashing gargantuan trees for food, and met with their deaths in the dismal swamps of an unknown age. These weird creatures haunted me in my dreams for a long time after I heard about them.

I received a beautiful shell once, and I learned how a tiny mollusc had built that lustrous coil to reside in. My teacher also taught me how the shell-building process of the molluscs symbolises the development of the mind. Just as the mantle of the Nautilus transforms the material it absorbs from the water and makes it a part of itself,

similarly the parts of knowledge that one gathers witness change to be transformed into pearls of thought. I learned how the Nautilus sails on the blue waters of the Indian Ocean in his 'ship of pearl'. I learned about the children of the sea, like how the little polyps built the lovely coral isles of the Pacific, amid waves that dashed upon them.

Once, the growth of a plant formed the text of a lesson. We purchased a lily, setting it in a sunny window. Soon, the green pointed buds displayed signs of opening. The slim, finger-like leaves on the outside opened slowly, albeit reluctantly. The loveliness that was hidden was revealed in a systematic process. Always, there was one bud that was larger and lovelier than the rest, which pushed her outer covering back with more pride and glory. It was as if she knew that she was the lily-queen, not reticent like her other sisters, who revealed themselves shyly in comparison. Then, the whole plant was a nodding picture of beauty and fragrance.

Eleven tadpoles in a glass globe were once set in a window full of plants as I eagerly discovered all about them. It was a whole lot of fun to dip my hand into the bowl to feel the tadpoles frisk here and there through my fingers. Once, an ambitious tadpole jumped out of the bowl to his apparent death on the floor, a slight flicker of his tail being the only sign of life. But he was back to his elements as soon as he was released into the water again, swimming in circles joyously. He had made his great leap, seen the world, and was now content to bask in his glasshouse till he attained his status of froghood. When he did so, he went to reside in the leafy pool at the end of the garden, making the summer-nights musical with his renditions of everlasting love songs.

So, I learned from life itself. My teacher unfolded and developed the mass of possibilities that I, Helen Keller, was. Miss Sullivan always pointed out the beauty in everything, and never stopped trying in thought, action and example to make my life meaningful, lovely, and useful.

Thanks to her love, foresight and genius, the first phase of my education was so beautiful. Realising that a child's mind is like a shallow brook, she fed it relentlessly with the water of mountain streams and hidden springs till it developed into a deep river.

Any teacher can take a child to the classroom, but not every teacher can make a child learn. The child will only work in happiness when at liberty. Both the pleasure of victory and the pain of failure must be experienced before distasteful tasks are attempted by the child willingly. Only then will a child dance bravely through the routine monotony of textbook learning.

My teacher is so close to me that I can barely think that she is apart from me. I don't know if my delight in all beautiful things is natural or it is because of her influence. But I know that we are inseparable as beings, and that every step that I take in life is hers. My best belongs to her, and everything that has been aroused in me, be it talent, aspiration, or happiness, is because of her.

Chapter Eight

Christmas

The first Christmas after Miss Sullivan arrived at our house was a grand event. Although everyone in my family planned surprises for me, what pleased me the most was that Miss Sullivan and I planned surprises for everyone else, together. The mystery revolving around Christmas gifts was my greatest happiness and pleasure. My friends excited my curiosity further by dropping hints and forming half-spelled sentences that they held back fully at the height of suspense. Miss Sullivan and I kept up the guessing game which enhanced my language skills more than any set of lessons.

We played our guessing game every evening, seated around a blazing fire. As Christmas approached, this guessing game reached a state of feverish excitement.

The Tuscumbia schoolchildren invited me to their Christmas tree on Christmas Eve. The beautiful tree shone prettily, illuminated in the soft light, the branches laden with strangely wonderful fruit. It was a moment of ecstatic happiness as I danced and skipped around the tree. I was ecstatic upon knowing that each child would receive a Christmas gift, and that I was chosen to hand over their gifts to them. I was so happy in this new role that I did not even bother to look at my own gifts that I had received. I was content with the gift from this tree and to leave all other gifts I had received till morning.

That night, after hanging my stocking, I lay awake for a long time. Pretending to be asleep, I awaited Santa Claus to see what he would do when he arrived. Finally, I fell asleep with a white bear and a new doll in my arms. I woke up the entire family with a shout of 'Merry Christmas!' the following morning.

I discovered surprises not just in the stockings, but everywhere; on the chairs, table, at the door, and on the window-sill. I could barely walk without stumbling on a bit of Christmas wrapped up in tissue paper. But my joy reached new heights when Miss Sullivan gifted me a canary. Little Tim was so tame that he would hop on my little finger and even eat out of my hand. Miss Sullivan taught me how to take care of my new pet, and every morning after breakfast, I prepared his bath, cleaned his cage, and filled his cups with fresh seed and water.

One morning, I left Little Tim's cage on the window-sill as I fetched water for his bath. Upon my return, I felt a big cat brush past me just as I had opened the door. Initially, I did not realise what had happened; but when I put my hand in Little Tim's cage, and his pretty wings did not respond to my touch and his small claws did not grab my finger, I knew that I would never see my sweet little singer ever again.

Chapter Nine

Travelling to Boston

The journey to Boston in May 1888 was the next most important event in my life. How different this trip was from the one I had embarked on to Baltimore two years ago! I had transformed from being that restless, attention seeking creature on the train. Sitting quietly by the car window now, I absorbed everything Miss Sullivan told me she saw outside. She described the lovely Tennessee River, the great cotton-fields, the woods and the hills, and the throng of laughing people at the stations, waving to the passengers and selling mouth-watering candy and popcorn balls.

Nancy, my big rag doll, sat opposite me in a new dress and a sun bonnet, staring at me with her beady eyes. As I was absorbed in my teacher's narrative, I ignored Nancy totally. I hid my guilt by pretending that Nancy was asleep. Soon after we arrived in Boston, Nancy was covered in dirt, thanks to the mud-pies I had forced down her throat, despite her not displaying any liking for them. The laundress at the Perkins Institution carried off Nancy for a bath. Poor Nancy could not take all this pressure and was reduced to a formless pile of cotton when I saw her next.

As soon as we had reached the Perkins Institute for the Blind, I started making friends with the blind children there. I was thrilled to discover that they knew the manual alphabet. It was sheer joy to interact with my own kind; children who knew my language. Till now, I had felt like a foreigner conversing with the aid of an interpreter. Here, I was in my own country and it took me some time to appreciate the fact

that all my new friends here were blind. I recall the surprise and sadness when they placed their hands lovingly over mine when I spoke to them and they told me that they read books with their fingers. This did come as a surprise, as I had expected that they would be blessed with a sort of 'second sight' just because they could hear although they were blind. But all of them were so happy and contented that I lost all my sadness in the pleasure of their company.

Just a day in the company of my blind friends made me feel totally at home in a new environment. I anticipated pleasant experiences one after another as the days flew by. I could not bring myself to believe that the world was a huge one as for me, it was Boston that was the beginning and the end of creation. We visited Bunker Hill during our Boston trip, and I received my first lesson in history there. I was very excited as I was told the tale of the brave soldiers who had fought on the same ground where we stood.

We travelled to Plymouth by water the next day. My first trip on the ocean involved my first voyage in a steamboat as well. But I began crying as I mistook the rumbling of the steamboat machine to be thunder. I feared that it would start raining and spoil our outdoor picnic. What interested me most about Plymouth was the great rock on which the pilgrims landed. I could touch the rock, and that would make the arrival of the pilgrims and their great deeds even more real in my mind. A kind gentleman had gifted me a miniature model of the Plymouth Rock at Pilgrim Hall, and I have often held it in my hand. I have felt its curves, the split in the centre and the embossed '1620' on it.

I knew the wonderful story of the great pilgrims and marvelled at their bravery and generosity despite seeking a home in a new land. I was under the impression that they desired the freedom of their fellow men as well as their own. Imagine my disappointment and surprise when I was aware of their acts of

persecution later, that make us recoil in shame. Isn't it ironic that we revel in the bravery and energy that gifted us our 'Country Beautiful'?

Mr William Endicott and his daughter were among the friends I had made in Boston. Their kindness gave birth to several fond memories. We visited their lovely home in Beverly Farms one day. I was so happy exploring their rose-garden and playing with their dogs, little curly-haired Fritz with long ears, and big Leo who made friends with me. I recall how Nimrod, the speediest of all horses, nestled his nose into my hands to be petted, and for a lump of sugar. I also recall the beach, where I played in the sand for the first time in my life. Mr Endicott told me tales about those massive ships that sailed from Boston and travelled to Europe. I met the man many times after that, and he was always kind to me, and a good friend. I think it was because of him that I renamed the city of Boston as 'the City of Kind Hearts'.

Chapter Ten

The Ocean and the Woods

Before the Perkins Institute shut down for the summer, it was decided that Miss Sullivan and I would go to Brewster, on Cape Cod to spend our vacation, accompanied by our dear friend, Mrs Hopkins. I was elated, as my mind revisited the lovely stories I had heard about the sea.

I had lived my entire life far inland without even a whiff of salt air. But the description of the ocean in a big book called 'Our World' had always made me long to touch the mighty sea and feel it roar. Now that my dream was about to come true, my little heart danced with joy.

As soon as I was helped into my bathing suit, I jumped upon the warm sand, and without much thought or fear, plunged into the cool water. The sensation filled me with great joy. But this elation soon gave way to terror as my foot hit a rock suddenly and water rushed over my head. I flung my hands about for support, clutching at the water and seaweed. But all my efforts were in vain! It was as if the waves were playing a game with me, tossing me about in great fun and frolic. I was horrified as the earth had slipped from my feet.

Thankfully, the sea decided to have mercy on me, and threw me back on the shore as if it had tired itself of its new toy. My teacher clasped me in her arms instantly in a loving embrace.

"Who put salt in the water?" I demanded instantly, as soon as I had recovered from my shock. After this initial disappointment with the sea, I decided to sit on a big rock in my bathing suit and feel the waves dash against it

with periodic regularity. As I did so, showers of spray covered me as the waves fell on the rock with all their might, rocking the entire beach with their onslaught. I clung to the rock, fascinated and tense at the same time.

One day, Miss Sullivan drew my attention towards a strange object she had captured from the shallow water. It was a giant horseshoe crab, and I thought it was strange that he carried his house on his back.

What a delightful pet he will make, I thought, as I grabbed him by his tail, and carried him home. He was heavy indeed, and it took all my strength to drag him half a mile. I pestered Miss Sullivan till she agreed to place the crab in a trough near a well where I was sure he'd be safe. But the next morning, he had vanished! No one knew where he had gone, or how he had escaped. I was greatly dejected initially but came to realise that it was not right to imprison this poor creature and alienate him from his natural environment. Hence, the thought that

he had returned to sea, made me happy later.

I returned to my southern home in autumn with a heart full of happy memories and experiences. That began my resurrection of sorts, as the treasures of a brand-new world were suddenly revealed to me. I met so many people who spelled into my hand, and the wide empty spaces between my mind and the mind of others bloomed like a rose.

The autumn months were spent with my family at our summer cottage which was located atop a mountain, 14 miles from Tuscumbia. This was named 'Fern Quarry' because of an abandoned limestone quarry in its proximity. Three merry little streams ran straight through it, descending from springs in the rocks above. The opening was full of ferns that totally covered the limestone beds, also hiding the streams here and there. The rest of the mountain was thickly wooded with massive oaks and resplendent evergreens that boasted of trunks like mossy pillars. Garlands of ivy and mistletoe

descended from the branches and the fragrance of persimmon trees lingered in every nook and corner of the wood. This sweet fragrance set the heart at ease. Wild muscadine and scuppernong vines swung from tree to tree in some areas, frequented by beautiful butterflies and buzzing insects. During the late afternoon, it was lovely to lose ourselves in the woods and to breathe in the fresh air.

Our cottage was a rough camp of sorts, strategically located on the top of the mountain, amidst oaks and pines. There was a long open hall with small rooms arranged on each side of it. A wide piazza was round the house. Here, the mountain winds blew, carrying sweet wood-scents. We spent most of our time at the piazza, eating, working and playing. A huge butternut tree was at the back door, and the steps had been constructed round it. In front, the trees were so close that I could touch them to feel the wind giving their branches a shake.

Fern Quarry received many visitors. In the evening, the men played cards by the campfire and talked about sports and other topics. They exchanged fishing and hunting stories, involving catching the most elusive fish, outrunning the fastest deer or hunting the wiliest of foxes. They spoke with so much confidence that I was convinced that animals like the lion and the tiger were no match for these experienced hunters.

The smell of coffee, the rattling of guns and the heavy footsteps of the men woke me up at the crack of dawn. I sensed horses stamping about, which belonged to these hunters. The horses had carried the men from town and were tied to the trees all night as they neighed loudly, eager to set off. At last the men mounted the horses, and the party rode off with loud cries of "with hark, whoop, and wild halloo".

We decided to make a barbecue later in the morning. We kindled a fire at the bottom of a deep hole. Then, big sticks were laid crosswise

at the top, from which meat was hung and turned on spits. The tempting smell of the meat made me hungry even before the food was served.

The hunting party made its appearance just as the barbecue preparations had reached its zenith. They struggled and stumbled, and were hot and exhausted. The horses were fatigued and so were the dogs. But there wasn't a single kill! Each hunter declared that he had seen at least one deer, and that the animal had come within handshaking distance. But sadly, the deer disappeared as soon as the guns were aimed. The hunters soon overcame their disappointment as we sat down together to enjoy a meal of veal and roast pig.

One summer, I had my own pony at Fern Quarry. I named him Black Beauty after the character in the famous book, as he resembled his namesake in every possible manner, right from the glossy black coat to the white star on his forehead. Many of my treasured moments

were spent riding Black Beauty. Miss Sullivan would often let go of the leading-rein, and the pony trotted or stopped to chew on the grass as he wished. When I did not wish to ride, my teacher and I would get lost in the woods after breakfast, returning to the cottage with arms full of ferns, goldenrod, laurel and lovely swamp-flowers that are typically characteristic of the South. Besides collecting flowers, we also went nutting with Mildred and my little cousins. I helped them open the chestnut burrs and break the shells of big, sweet walnuts and hickory-nuts.

A railroad was present at the base of the mountain, where the children watched the trains go by speedily. The sound of a loud whistle made us rush to the steps one day, and an excited Mildred informed me that a cow or horse had strayed onto the tracks. Approximately a mile away, lay a trestle spanning a deep gorge, and it was difficult to cross over because the ties were wide apart and narrow. It was almost like walking on thin knives! I had never crossed this until one day Miss Sullivan, Mildred and I were lost in the woods. We wandered for hours without finding a way back home.

"There's the trestle!" Mildred suddenly exclaimed.

Ideally, we would not have chosen to take such a precarious path, but it was getting dark and late and the trestle offered a short cut to reach home. I had to feel for the rails with my toe but was not scared. I was doing fine till I heard a faint 'puff, puff' from the distance.

"It's the train!" Mildred yelled, and the train would have been upon us if we hadn't climbed down on the crossbraces immediately. As the train rushed over our heads, I felt the engine's hot breath on my face. The smoke and ashes from the locomotive almost choked us. The trestle shook like a trembling leaf in the wind as the train stormed by, and I thought we would be dashed to our deaths. With great difficulty, we found the track again. Reaching home way after dark, we discovered that the cottage was empty. Everyone in the family was out looking for us!

Chapter Eleven

Stormy Days

Most of my winters were now spent in the North after my first visit to Boston. Once, I visited a New England village characterised by huge snow fields and frozen lakes. The treasures of the snow were now fully revealed to me. Imagine my surprise on discovering that a mysterious hand had stripped the bushes and the trees, with a few wrinkled leaves here and there. The birds had flown away, and their bare nests were filled with snow. The earth had been numbed by winter's icy touch, and his presence was everywhere. The very spirits of the trees had

shrunk to their roots, and they lay there, fast asleep. Even when the sun shone, there was a lack of warmth!

In the forest of icicles, a snowstorm arrived one day. We rushed outside to see the first snowflakes descending. A snowy night shut out the world after hours of silent snowfall, and in the morning, the entire landscape was not recognisable at all. The roads were hidden with not a single landmark visible. One could only see trees rising from a wasteland of snow.

A wind from the northeast arrived unannounced in the evening, and the snowflakes moved here and there furiously. We sat around the great fire telling happy stories, trying to shut out the depressing weather and the solitude that cut off our communication with the outside world. But in the night, the wind howled with such fury that we were filled with great terror. The branches of the trees near the house rattled the window panes as the rafters creaked and strained.

After three days, the storm ceased, and the snowfall died down. The sun came out to shine brightly over the plain. Narrow paths were shovelled through the drifts, and I went out after putting on my cloak and hood. The air stung my cheeks like fire. The trees stood silently like white marble figures and the sweet odour of the pine-needles seemed to have evaporated. The twigs of the trees sparkled like diamonds as the rays of the sun fell on them. But they crumbled to the ground as soon as they were touched.

The light was so dazzling that it almost penetrated the darkness that veiled my eyes. But the drifts slowly shrunk with each passing day. But before they had totally disappeared, another storm arrived ensuring I was indoors all of winter. The lake lay hard and frozen beneath the sun.

Tobogganing was our favourite amusement that winter. In certain areas, the shore of the lake rose abruptly from the edge of the water.

We used to coast down these steep slopes by getting on our toboggan. A boy would give us a shove, and off we would go! We would plunge through drifts and jumping hollows as we would swoop down the lake. Shooting across the shiny surface to the opposite bank, we would bask in the thrill and excitement of tobogganing. In a wild, glad moment, we would snap the link of the chain that bound us to the earth as we joined hands with the wind.

Chapter Twelve

Learning to Speak

I learned to speak in the spring of 1890. The ability to make inaudible sounds had always been a part of me. I made noises keeping one hand on my throat while the other hand felt my lip movements. I was happy with everything that created a noise and loved feeling the dog bark and the cat purr. I loved keeping a hand on a singer's throat or on the piano as it was being played. Before I lost my ability to see and hear, I was rapidly making progress in speech. But it was concluded after my illness that I had stopped talking simply because I had ceased to hear.

I did make many sounds and words though, more because of exercising my vocal cords rather than a means of communication. But I remembered the meaning of one word, 'water', although I pronounced it as 'wa-wa'. But even this became less comprehensible until Miss Sullivan began teaching me. After I learned how to spell the word on my fingers, I stopped using this pronunciation.

I was aware that people around me used a form of communication that was very different from mine, and I was aware of the dissatisfaction of this form even before I realised that a deaf child could be taught to speak. A person dependent on the manual alphabet always has a restrained, narrow sense. I was becoming agitated because of these thoughts, and I continued using my lips and voice to communicate. My friends advised me against this, fearful that it would lead to further disappointment. But I continued, and soon, an accident took place that resulted in breaking down this great wall–I heard the story of Ragnhild Kaata.

In 1890, Mrs Lamson, who had taught Laura Bridgman, arrived to see me, and told me the story of Ragnhild Kaata, a deaf and blind girl in Norway, who had actually been taught to speak. I was burning with eagerness after I heard this story and resolved firmly that I would learn how to speak. My teacher took me to seek Miss Sarah Fuller's advice and help. She was the principal of the Horace Mann School and was a lovely, sweet-natured lady. She offered to teach me how to speak and the lessons began on 26 March 1890.

Miss Fuller passed my hand lightly over her face, allowing me to feel the position of her tongue and lips when she uttered a sound. This was her simple method. I was anxious to imitate her every action and had picked up six elements of speech: M, P, A, S, T, and I, in just an hour. She gave me eleven lessons, and I was elated and surprised when I managed to utter my first connected sentence, "It is warm." Although they were broken and stammered syllables, they were human speech after all. A deaf child who has earnestly tried to speak words which he or she has never heard is like one emerging from the prison of silence. No tone of love or song of bird or sound of music can penetrate the stillness of this oppressive prison. Imagine the thrill and surprise and the joy of discovery the child experiences upon uttering his or her first word! My elation can perhaps be gauged by the way I started talking to my toys, the trees, birds, and animals. I was overjoyed when Mildred ran towards me at my call and when the dogs followed my commands. To be able to speak without needing an interpreter was a godsend and a boon, and happy thoughts emerged from my mind whenever I spoke.

But one must not suppose that I could talk fluently at this early stage as I had only picked up the elements of speech. The truth was that Miss Fuller and Miss Sullivan understood what I

was saying, but most people couldn't. I also did not do the rest of the work myself after learning the elements of speech. I wouldn't have been where I am now but for Miss Sullivan's untiring perseverance, devotion and sheer genius.

To perfect natural speech, I toiled night and day before my best friends understood what I was trying to say. Miss Sullivan's constant assistance was needed for me to articulate each sound distinctly and to merge all sounds in a thousand ways. Till date, she brings my attention to mispronounced words. Only the teachers of the deaf will be able to understand my difficult position. I only had my fingers to rely on to read my teacher's lips, and catching the vibrations of the throat, mouth movements and facial expressions by mere touch was not easy. This sense was mostly faulty, and I had to repeat the words or sentences for hours sometimes whenever this happened, until the proper sound emerged. It was practice, practice and more practice!

I was discouraged and fatigued often, but what spurred me on was the desire for success and the idea of pleasing my loved ones with my achievements.

My little sister will know what I am saying now! was a thought that was stronger than all the hurdles I faced.

"I am not dumb now!" I repeated happily as the thought struck me that talking was much easier than having to spell the words with your fingers. I abandoned the manual alphabet as a tool of communication immediately, but Miss Sullivan and a few of my friends still use this when they speak to me today, simply because it is faster and more convenient than lip-reading.

I should explain how we use the manual alphabet as it is puzzling for people who do not know us properly. A person reading or talking to me spells with his hand, using the single-hand manual alphabet used normally by the deaf. I place my hand on the speaker's hand lightly so that the movements are not

disturbed. The hand position is as easy to feel as it is to see. I feel each letter as easily as you see it and the fingers are greatly flexible thanks to constant practice. Some of my friends spell as fast as a typewriter expert's writing speed.

After I had conquered basic speech, I could not wait to go home. I made my way home, constantly talking to Miss Sullivan to improve more. When the train rolled into Tuscumbia station, my entire family was waiting for me on the platform. My eyes well up in tears now when I think about how my mother hugged me with delight, speechless as she shook and trembled. She took in every syllable I uttered, as little Mildred held my other hand, kissing it and dancing in joy. My father expressed his pride and love in a stoic silence. It was as if Isaiah's prophecy had come true.

Helen

Chapter Thirteen

The Frost King

The winter of 1892 darkened my childhood happiness with a single cloud. I lived in a long period of fear, anxiety and self-doubt. I lost my love for books, and when I think of those days now, it chills my heart.

I had written a short story titled, 'The Frost King', and had sent it to Mr Anagnos, of the Perkins Institution for the Blind. This story was the root of all the trouble, and I had written it when I was at home the autumn after I had learned to speak. At Fern Quarry, Miss Sullivan had described to me the beauties of the late foliage, and this description triggered the

memory of a story which had been read out to me sometime. I must have retained this story in my subconsciousness, and I was unaware of this when I was 'making up my story'.

So, I wrote sentence after sentence on my braille slate and after the story was finished, I read it out to my teacher. I remember being briefly annoyed when she corrected the pronunciation of a word. I also recall reading it aloud at dinner to my assembled family. They were surprised that I wrote so well, and someone even asked me if I had read the story somewhere. This question surprised me, as I did not have any memory of this story being read to me.

"No, it is my story," I insisted. "I have written it for Mr Anagnos."

It was suggested that I change the title of the story from 'Autumn Leaves' to 'The Frost King'. I did so and sent the story to Mr Anagnos on his birthday, who was delighted with my work. He also published it in one of the Perkins Institution

reports, taking my happiness to a supreme level. But I was soon dashed to earth when a startling discovery was made– a story called 'The Frost Fairies' by Miss Margaret T. Canby had been published in a book called 'Birdie and His Friends' much before I had been born. The two stories were so strikingly similar in content and language that it was clear that 'The Frost Fairies' had been read out to me sometime and I had plagiarised it, albeit unknowingly.

I was stunned! *What a disgrace I was,* I thought. The people who loved me now regarded me suspiciously. But how could I have done something like this? I struggled to remember anything that I had read about frost previously and could only recall Jack Frost and a poem for children titled, 'The Freaks of the Frost'.

Although Mr Anagnos was greatly worried initially, he believed what I had to say and was so kind to me that my clouds of gloom almost disappeared. I tried to be happy to please

him and made myself as pretty as possible to celebrate Washington's birthday, which was soon after I received the sad news. The night before the celebration, one of the teachers of the institution questioned me regarding 'The Frost King' and in my reply, she detected a confession that I recalled Miss Canby's story titled 'The Frost Fairies'. She laid her findings before Mr Anagnos immediately, although I categorically told her that she was mistaken. Mr Anagnos, who was rather fond of me, refused to believe me and was convinced that Miss Sullivan and I had plagiarised someone else's thoughts in order to impress him.

I was presented before a court of investigation made up of teachers and officials of the institution, and Miss Sullivan was asked to leave the room. Then, I was grilled with persistent questions, the sole objective of which was to force me to admit that I recalled having 'The Frost Fairies' read aloud to me. I sensed that all of them were suspicious and even

loving friends looked at me with reproach. My heart beat like a drum, and I could only speak in monosyllables. I suffered deep inside even though it was only a mistake on my part that I did not even realise. When I left the room finally, I was too dazed to even realise my teacher's caresses or the kind words of my friends, who said that I was a brave girl and they were proud of me. I wept in bed that night, and the thought of death before the morning arrived, comforted me greatly. I think my spirit would have been shattered beyond repair had this incident taken place when I was much older. But because I was so young, the angel of forgetfulness managed to make the bitter memories and sadness disappear in time.

Miss Sullivan had never heard of 'The Frost Fairies', or the book in which it was published. With the aid of Dr Alexander Graham Bell, she began investigating the matter, and soon reached her deductions. It appeared that Mrs Sophia C. Hopkins possessed a copy of Miss

Canby's book, 'Birdie and His Friends' in 1888, the same year we spent the summer with her at Brewster. Mrs Hopkins told me later that she had tried to read me several books while Miss Sullivan was away, and she was sure that 'Birdie and His Friends' was one of them. Sadly, the book had disappeared when she sold her house and disposed of several juvenile books. 'Birdie and His Friends' was one of those books she had given away.

I was a small child then, and barely remember the reading of these stories. But it is for sure that the language was effectively embossed on my brain when those stories were read to me, although no one knew this till this date, including myself. People were kind to me during this difficult time and I received many sympathetic messages. Miss Canby herself wrote me a kind note, saying, "You will write a great story out of your own head someday, and that will be a great help and comfort to many".

But somehow, this prophecy has never

come true! I have never endeavoured to play with words again except for the pleasure of it. But also, I have been gripped by the fear that what I write is not my original work. Even attempting to write a letter to my mother would seize me with terror, and I would check the sentences repeatedly to ensure that they hadn't been taken from a book. If not for the constant encouragement of Miss Sullivan, I think I would have given up writing altogether.

When I read 'The Frost Stories' much later, I realised that I had borrowed heavily from it. Phrases describing golden autumn leaves as 'Yes, they are beautiful enough to comfort us for the flight of summer' were taken directly from Miss Canby's story. I realised that I had this habit of gathering what pleased me, and penning it down as my own. This habit forms a major part of my initial attempts at correspondence and writing. I realised that I had also borrowed heavily from different sources when I wrote about the old cities of Italy and Greece.

Like every other young inexperienced person, I was also learning through assimilation and imitation as I tried to put my thoughts into ideas and then into words. Everything I discovered in books that pleased me were driven into my memory bank either consciously or subconsciously till I adapted it. As Stevenson rightly put it, "the young writer instinctively tries to copy whatever seems admirable, and then shifts his admiration with incredible versatility. Only after years of practice do great men and women master the legion of words."

I haven't completed this process yet, sadly. I am positive that I cannot distinguish my own thoughts from the ones that I read. Whatever I read and like form the very thought of my mind. My compositions are made up of my own crude notions and are polished with the brighter thoughts of authors I have admired. Possibly, the greatest difficulty of writing is to express our confused ideas, partial thoughts and feelings with the language of the educated mind. It's like

THE STORY OF MY LIFE
HELEN KELLER
THE STORY OF MY LIFE
HELEN KELLER

trying to put a Chinese puzzle together, where the words are not fitting in the spaces or not matching the design. But we keep trying as we are not ready to concede defeat where others have succeeded. "There is no way to become original, except to be born so," says Stevenson. I know that I might not be original, but I do hope to make my amateurish, artificial compositions much better in terms of originality. This way, my own thoughts and experiences will emerge from the depths. In a way, this bitter experience did me good as it made me realise the problems in my composition. Sadly, it also resulted in the loss of a dear friend, Mr Anagnos.

After 'The Story of My Life' was published, Mr Anagnos had made a statement in a letter to Mr Macy. He believed I was innocent. But whatever the case might have been, there is no denying the fact that a loving atmosphere had suddenly changed in that room to a hostile and threatening one, and the events that followed proved this. Mr Anagnos believed that Miss

The Frost
Stories

Sullivan and I were innocent for as long as two years, and then suddenly changed his opinion about us for reasons unknown. The account of 'The Frost King' has been given by me only because it was instrumental in shaping my life and education. To avoid any misunderstanding, I have stated the facts exactly as they appear to me, without the notion of blaming anyone or defending myself.

Chapter Fourteen

Preparing for College

After the 'Frost King' incident, I spent the following summer and winter in Alabama with my family. I was so happy that the bitterness was forgotten. The ground was paved with the crimson and golden leaves of autumn, and the musk-scented grapes at the end of the garden were turning golden brown in the sunshine.

A year after I had written 'The Frost King', I began work on a sketch of my life. I was still haunted by the fact that whatever I wrote might not be my own thoughts, and no one was aware of this fear except Miss Sullivan. Whenever a new idea flashed in my head, I would break it

out softly to my teacher, first saying, "I am sure it is not mine!"

A strange fear gnawed at my heart whenever I finished writing a paragraph.

What if this was written by someone long ago? I thought, and I could not write anymore on that day. Even today, I experience such moments of self-doubt and uneasiness. Miss Sullivan tried her best to comfort and encourage me, but the terrible experience I had encountered had left a lasting impression on my mind. It was to restore my self-confidence that Miss Sullivan proposed that I write a sketch of my life for the Youth's Companion. I was just 12 years old, and I began writing in a shy and fearful manner. Yet, I wrote purposefully, goaded on by my teacher.

The main events of my life of the year 1893 were my trip to Washington during the inauguration ceremony of President Cleveland, trips to Niagara, and the World's Fair. Such visits ensured that my studies were interrupted constantly and put on the backburner for many

weeks. So, penning down a connected account of them was impossible.

We visited Niagara in March 1893, and I cannot describe my emotions when I stood on the point overhanging the American Falls. I could feel the earth shake and the air vibrate! People found it strange that I was affected by the wonderous beauty of the Niagara.

"What does this beauty mean to you?" they are always asking. "You can neither see the waves nor hear their roar!"

Well, in a sense they mean everything! But I cannot decipher or understand this meaning any more than I can fathom concepts like love, religion or goodness.

Miss Sullivan and I visited the World's Fair accompanied by Dr Alexander Graham Bell in the summer of 1893. It was delightful for me to experience a thousand childhood fantasies transformed into realities. I made a trip around the world in my imagination every day, experiencing marvels of invention, industry and

skill, as all the activities of human life were right under my fingertips.

The Midway Plaisance appeared like the 'Arabian Nights', and I loved visiting here. I found the India of my books in its strange bazaar with its Shiva and Elephant God. I found a model of Cairo focussing on the Pyramids, mosques, and camel processions. The lagoons of Venice featured the city and fountains. I pretended to board a Viking ship, and played at being a seaman. A model of the Santa Maria was there a little distance away from the model of the Viking ship. The captain showed me Columbus's cabin and his desk with the hour-glass on it. This small instrument was impressive as I thought how the heroic navigator must have felt watching the sand drop grain by grain even as his enemies were plotting to kill him.

Mr Higginbotham, president of the World's Fair, kindly permitted me to touch the exhibits, and I attacked Peru with the eagerness of Pizarro. I soaked in the glories of the fair with

my fingers, and everything was fascinating, especially the French bronzes. They were so lifelike that it seemed the artist had captured angel visions to bind them in earthly forms.

I learned about the process of mining diamonds at the Cape of Good Hope exhibit. I felt the moving machinery whenever possible to get a clearer idea as to how the stones were weighed, cut and polished. Dr Bell accompanied us everywhere here and explained the objects of interest in greater detail to me. We examined the telephones, autophones, phonographs and other inventions in the electrical buildings, and he explained to me how a message was sent on wires with great speed, and how it was possible to draw fire from the sky just like Prometheus.

The relics of ancient Mexico were very interesting in the anthropological department, and so were the Egyptian mummies, which I resisted from touching. From these relics, I learned more about the progress of man than any book or sermon has taught me. These

experiences also strengthened my vocabulary, and the three weeks I spent at the fair enhanced a small child's interest from fairy tales and toys to the appreciation of important things in the real world.

Prior to October 1893, I had studied several subjects in isolation like the histories of Greece, Rome and the United States. I also had a French grammar in raised print, and armed with the knowledge of a little French, amused myself in playing with French words to compose some work. I also tried to master the French pronunciation on my own on a rainy day, and thanks to works like La Fontaine's Fables, 'Le Medecin Malgre Lui', and passages from 'Athalie', I gathered a fair knowledge of French.

I also devoted enough time to improve my speech, reading aloud to Miss Sullivan and reciting the works of my favourite poets which I had memorised. She helped me by correcting my pronunciation and to phrase and inflect better. But only after the visit to the World's Fair, did

I have lessons in special subjects at fixed hours. At the time, Miss Sullivan and I were visiting the family of Mr William Wade in Hulton, Pennsylvania. Mr Irons, their neighbour, was a good Latin scholar, and it was arranged to have me study under him. He was an experienced man with a kind nature. Mainly, he taught me Latin grammar, but often helped me in arithmetic, which I hated as it was problematic. He also read with me 'In Memoriam' by Tennyson. I had read several books before, but never from a critical point of view. For the first time, I learned how to know an author and to recognise his distinct style of writing.

Initially, I was reluctant to study Latin grammar. It was absurd to waste time by analysing each word when its meaning was clear in the first place. But as we delved deeper into the subject, it became more interesting and the beauty of the language captivated me. I amused myself by reading Latin passages, and I enjoy this pastime till date.

There is nothing more beautiful than the images and sentiments that are presented by a language one has been just introduced to as it shapes the mind with beautiful thoughts. Miss Sullivan sat beside me during my lessons, spelling into my hand whatever Mr Irons said as well as looking up new words for me. When I went home to Alabama, I had just started reading Caesar's 'Gallic War'.

THE AMERICAN ASSOCIATION
PRESENTS A MEETING TO
PROMOTE THE TEACHING OF
SPEECH TO THE
CHAUTAUQUA 1894

Chapter Fifteen

Wright-Humason

I attended the meeting of the American Association to Promote the Teaching of Speech to the Deaf at Chautauqua in the summer of 1894. Then, it was decided that I would leave for New York to attend the Wright-Humason School for the Deaf. It was October 1894 when I left with Miss Sullivan. This school was selected to gain the highest advantages in vocal culture and training in lip-reading. During my two years tenure in this school, I also studied physical geography, arithmetic, German and French.

My German teacher was named Miss Reamy, and she could use the manual alphabet too. After I had gained a substantial vocabulary, the two of us spoke in German whenever we could. In a few months, I could understand almost whatever she said. I read 'Wilhelm Tell' before the end of my first year here, and I think I made more progress in German than any of the other subjects here. Strangely, I had more difficulty with French. But this was because Madame Olivier, my French teacher did not know the manual alphabet. Hence, she gave her lessons orally and I could not read her lips as easily. So, my progress in French was slower than German. But I did manage to read 'Le Medicin Malgre Lui' again. It was great fun, but I did not like it as much as 'Wilhelm Tell'.

My progress in lip-reading and speech was not as rapid as my teachers and I had hoped it to be. My ambition to speak like other people could not be reached, and I think my teachers and I set our targets too high, and hence,

disappointment was inevitable. Arithmetic was still as troublesome, and I chose guessing over reasoning, which was dangerous and increased my difficulties.

Despite my disappointments in these areas, I chased my other subjects with great zeal, especially physical geography. Learning the secrets of nature was delightful in the Old Testament's picturesque language–the winds blow from the four corners of the heavens, how the vapours ascend from the ends of the earth, how rivers are cut out among rocks, and how mountains are overturned. The two years in New York were happy indeed, and I revisit those moments with a smile. I recall the walks we took every day in Central Park, an area I found most beautiful and congenial in New York City.

In the spring, we made interesting excursions like sailing on the Hudson River and wandering about on its green banks. We also visited West Point, Tarrytown, Washington

Irving's home, where I took a walk through 'Sleepy Hollow'.

The teachers at Wright-Humason were always inclined to give all the pupils the advantages of those who hear enjoy. They tried hard to set them free from the cramping circumstances that ruled their lives.

Before I left New York, my happy days were clouded by the greatest sorrow that crept into my life. It was the saddest moment for me except for my father's death. Mr John P. Spaulding, of Boston, passed away in February 1896. Only those who knew and loved him can realise what the loss of this dear friend meant to me. He made everyone he met happy and was particularly kind towards Miss Sullivan and me. His death has left a void in our lives that has never been filled.

Chapter Sixteen

Cambridge

I entered the Cambridge School for Young Ladies in October 1896, to prepare for Radcliffe. When I was small, I visited Wellesley, surprising my friends by announcing, "Someday I shall go to college, and I shall attend Harvard!"

Upon being questioned why I wouldn't attend Wellesley my reply had been that there were only girls there. The desire to attend college was rooted deep in my mind, and after leaving New York, it became a purposeful thought. But the plan was to go to Cambridge as it was the nearest I could get to Harvard.

The plan for Cambridge School was to get

Miss Sullivan to attend classes with me and interpret the instructions. But my teachers had only taught normal pupils before this, and I could only converse with them after reading their lips. In the first year, I was studying English literature, English history, Latin, German, arithmetic, Latin composition, and occasional themes.

I had never undertaken a course of study before this with the intent of preparing for college. But thanks to Miss Sullivan, my English was perfect, and it was soon clear to my teachers that I needed no special instruction apart from the critical study of the books prescribed by the college. I had received a good start in French as well as six months of coaching in Latin. But German was the language I was most familiar with. Despite being blessed with these advantages, serious hurdles to my progress existed. It was impossible for Miss Sullivan to spell out in my hand what my books needed me to learn, and it was difficult to have textbooks

embossed so quickly to prove useful to my cause. My friends in London and Philadelphia were eager to have the work done for me quickly though.

I had to copy my Latin in braille for some time, so that I was able to recite with the other girls. Soon, my teachers became familiar with my imperfections of speech and could answer my questions and correct my mistakes easily. True, I was unable to take notes in class or write exercises; but I wrote all my compositions and translations on my typewriter after I reached home.

Every day, Miss Sullivan accompanied me to class, and patiently spelled out into my hand whatever the teachers said. During my study hours, she looked for new words for me to learn. She read and reread the books unavailable with me in raised print. The arduousness of her work is difficult to fathom.

My German instructor, Frau Grote, and the principal, Mr Gilman, were the only

teachers in the school who learned the finger alphabet so that they could instruct me. To give Miss Sullivan a little respite, the dear Frau Grote laboriously gave me special lessons twice a week.

I finished arithmetic that year, reviewed my Latin grammar, and read three chapters of Caesar's 'Gallic War'. In German, I read Schiller's 'Lied von der Glocke' and 'Taucher', Heine's 'Harzreise', Freytag's 'Aus dem Staat Friedrichs des Grossen', Riehl's 'Fluch Der Schonheit', Lessing's 'Minna von Barnhelm', and Goethe's 'Aus meinem Leben'. I loved reading these German books, especially the wonderful lyrics of Schiller, the history of Frederick the Great's amazing achievements, and the story of Goethe's life.

Mr Gilman instructed me partly in English literature. We read together 'As You Like It', Burke's 'Speech on Conciliation with America', and Macaulay's 'Life of Samuel Johnson'. Mr Gilman's profound knowledge of

history and literature, coupled with his clever explanations made my learning easier, simpler and happier. It was so much better than taking notes in classes.

Burke's speech taught me more about a political subject than any other book that I had read. I wondered as I read how King George and his ministers could have ignored his prophecy about their humiliation and our victory. As I admired Burke's mastery and eloquence, I thought how tragic it was that such gems of truth had been a victim of ignorance and corruption.

Macaulay's 'Life of Samuel Johnson' was interesting in a different way. My heart wept for the lonely man who was always kind despite suffering so much, and always helped the poor and the needy. I rejoiced at all his victories and shut my eyes to his faults. But despite Macaulay's brilliance and his skill to make the commonplace appear fresh and scenic, his positivity bored me at times.

At Cambridge, I enjoyed the companionship of girls my own age for the first time in my life. I lived in a pleasant house connected to the school with many others. I joined them in many games, including 'Blind Man's Bluff' and 'Frolics in the Snow'. We took long walks together and discussed our studies. A few girls learned how to speak to me as well, and it spared Miss Sullivan having to repeat their conversation to me.

My mother and my sister joined me for Christmas, and the kind Mr Gilman offered Mildred the opportunity to study in his school. Mildred and I were together for six happy months after that, helping each other study and playing together.

My preliminary examinations for Radcliffe took place from 29 June-3 July 1897. The subjects I offered were Elementary and Advanced German, Latin, French, English, and Greek and Roman history. The examinations totalled nine hours, and I passed in everything, receiving 'honours' in English and German.

The method of examination here required a student to pass in sixteen hours - twelve hours were elementary and four hours advanced. One had to pass five hours at a time to have them counted. The examination papers were handed out at Harvard at nine o'clock, and a special messenger fetched them to Radcliffe. Each candidate was known by a number and not by name. I was number 233, but as I had to use a typewriter, my identity could not be hidden. So, it was decided that I should take my examinations in a room all by myself as the noise of the typewriter could also disturb the other girls. Mr Gilman read all the papers to me using the manual alphabet, and a guard at the door prevented interruption.

Although it was difficult, I must confess that I haven't had this kind of advantage in any other examination after that. At Radcliffe, no one read the papers to me after they were written, and I had no chance to correct the errors unless I finished before the stipulated

time. So, I corrected only the mistakes I remembered making in the few minutes that were left with me after I finished.

There are two reasons why I passed with higher credit in the preliminaries than in the finals. No one read my work over to me in the finals, and in the preliminaries, the subjects were familiar to me. Mr Gilman also sent a certificate with my written work to the examiners, testifying that candidate number 233 had written the papers herself. I discovered that the preliminary examinations became easier and only the first one had been difficult. The day I was giving the Latin paper, Professor Schilling arrived to inform me that I had passed satisfactorily in German. That was a great encouragement indeed, and I went through my present ordeal with a light heart and a steady hand.

Chapter Seventeen

Gilman School

I was determined to succeed during my second year at Gilman school. But I encountered unforeseen difficulties in the first few weeks itself. Mr Gilman felt that I should study mathematics principally that year. Besides that, I had algebra, physics, geometry, astronomy, Latin and Greek. Unfortunately, many of the books I needed hadn't been embossed before my classes began. The classes I was in were huge, and it was not possible for my teachers to bestow special attention on me. Miss Sullivan was forced to read all the books for me and interpret for the teachers as well. For the first

time in eleven years, it appeared that Miss Sullivan would not be equal to the task.

Until I could purchase a braille writer, it was difficult for me to solve the problems in physics and write algebra and geometry in class. I couldn't follow the geometrical figures on the blackboard with my eyes, and the only way to know them clearly was to make them a cushion with straight and curved wires, having bent and pointed ends.

There were times when I lost all hope and courage. But slowly and steadily my troubles began to disappear. The embossed books and other apparatus arrived, and I immersed myself in my work diligently and confidently. Algebra and geometry were the only subjects that were elusive, despite my best efforts to comprehend them. But although I had no aptitude for mathematics, certain points were not fully or well explained to me as well. The geometrical diagrams were particularly irritating because I could not understand the relation the

different parts had with one another. Only after Mr Keith started teaching me, I had better clarity in mathematics.

I was trying to overcome these problems when something happened that changed everything. Just before the books arrived, Mr Gilman insisted to Miss Sullivan that I was being made to work too hard, and despite my earnest protests, he reduced the number of my recitations. Initially, it had been decided that I would need five years to prepare for college, but after seeing my progress, it was concluded that I would be ready in two years. Mr Gilman had agreed to this, but when he saw that my tasks were become puzzling for me, he declared that I was overworked. He insisted that I remain in his school for three more years. I did not agree to his plan as I wanted to enter college with my class.

I was unwell on 17th November and did not attend school. Miss Sullivan knew it was nothing serious, but Mr Gilman overreacted.

He concluded that I was breaking down and made alterations in my studies that would make it impossible for me to take my final examinations with my class. Finally, the differences of opinion between Mr Gilman and Miss Sullivan reached such proportions that my mother was forced to withdraw both me and my sister from the Cambridge school.

After some delay, I was put under the care of a tutor named Mr Merton S. Keith of Cambridge. Miss Sullivan and I spent the remainder of the winter with our friends, the Chamberlins in Wrentham, 25 miles away from Boston. Mr Keith arrived here to teach me twice a week from February to July 1898. He taught me geometry, algebra, Latin and Greek, while Miss Sullivan interpreted his instruction.

We returned to Boston in October 1898. In a span of eight months, I received lessons from Mr Keith five times a week, in hourly lessons. He patiently explained everything I hadn't understood in the previous lesson, gave me new work to do, and took home the Greek exercises I had done during the week on my typewriter. After correcting them at home, he returned them on his next visit.

This is how I prepared for college without interruption, and I found this private education easier and better than be taught in class. There was no rush and no confusion, and my tutor had a lot of time to explain to me whatever I did not comprehend. I worked faster and did better than what I did at school. Mathematics was still problematic, but Mr Keith even made mathematics interesting. He created small problems that my brain registered easily. Keeping my mind alert and keen, he trained it to reason clearly. I sought conclusions in a calm and logical manner now, instead of jumping to conclusions wildly. He was always gentle and kind, no matter how stupid or dull I was.

I took my final examinations for Radcliffe College in June 1899. Elementary Greek and Advanced Latin were scheduled on the

first day, while the second day had algebra, geometry and Advanced Greek.

Miss Sullivan was not permitted by the college authorities to read the examination papers to me. So, an instructor at the Perkins Institution for the Blind, Mr Vining, was given the responsibility to copy the papers for me in American braille. He was a stranger and could not communicate with me but for writing braille. The proctor was also a stranger and did not attempt to communicate with me either.

The braille worked fine enough in both languages, but problems emerged in geometry and algebra. I was perplexed, and averse to wasting precious time, especially in algebra. Although I was familiar with all literary braille commonly used in this country, namely English, American, and New York Point, I must mention that the several signs and symbols in algebra and geometry in the three systems are totally different. Sadly, I had used only English braille in my algebra.

Mr Vining had sent me a braille copy of one of the old Harvard papers in algebra two days before the examinations. To my dismay, I discovered that it was in the American notation. I instantly wrote to him, asking him to explain the signs. He sent me another paper and a table of signs, and I quickly sat down to learn the notations.

But the night before the algebra examination, as I struggled with some complicated examples, I realised I couldn't tell the combinations of bracket, brace and radical. Both Mr Keith and I were greatly worried and reached the college a little before the examination began. We had Mr Vining explain the American symbols fully.

The main problem I had with geometry was that I had always been used to reading the propositions in line print or have them spelled into my hand. Besides, I could not see what I wrote on my typewriter as I had always done my work in braille or in my head. Mr Keith had also taught me to solve problems mentally and

hadn't trained me to write examination papers. Hence, my work was excruciatingly slow, and I had to read the examples repeatedly before I could realise what I was supposed to do.

But I do not blame anyone. The administrative board of Radcliffe had no idea how difficult they were making my examinations, nor were they aware of the strange hurdles I had to encounter. But if they placed hurdles in my path unintentionally, I have the pleasure of knowing that I overcame them all!

Chapter Eighteen

Radcliffe

The struggle to enter college had concluded, and I could walk into Radcliffe whenever I pleased now. But it was decided that another year of study with Mr Keith would serve me well before I entered college. So, it was only in the fall of 1900 that my dream of attending college was realised.

The first day at Radcliffe was an interesting day and one I had looked forward to for years. I was aware of the obstacles ahead but was determined to overcome them. I took strength from the words of the wise Roman who said,

"To be banished from Rome is but to live outside of Rome."

I knew that my journey involved taking roads that were less frequented, and I eagerly began my studies. It was as if a brand new world were revealing itself to me, in all its beauty and light! I felt this desire to know everything. The professors in the lecture-halls were the very symbol of wisdom and knowledge.

But I soon realised that college was not the romantic environment that I had imagined. College had many disadvantages as well. The lack of time is the most prominent, as earlier, I had time to think and reflect. It appears that one attends college to learn, and not to think. Pleasures like solitude, books and imagination are abandoned in pursuit of knowledge.

I studied French, German, history, English composition and English literature in the first year. I read the French works of Corneille, Moliere, Racine, Alfred de Musset and Sainte-Beuve, and the German works of Goethe and Schiller.

In English literature, I critically studied Milton's poems and 'Areopagitica'.

In the classroom, I am almost all alone as the professor is so distant it is as if he is speaking through a telephone. The lectures are spelled into my hand as speedily as possible and I cannot even make notes like the other girls, jotting down whatever I remember when I reach home. I use the Hammond typewriter which is the best for my kind of work. Without the typewriter, I doubt if I could have attended college. Unfortunately, I do not have any free time like the other girls.

Last year, my second year at Radcliffe, I studied English composition. The Bible, the governments of America and Europe, the Odes of Horace, and Latin comedy were covered. The class in composition was the liveliest as the lectures were witty, interesting and exciting.

This year, I'm studying subjects that are closest to my heart like economics, Shakespeare,

Elizabethan literature, and the history of philosophy. But when it comes to studying the masters of literature, I have reservations about the innumerable comments and criticisms surrounding famous works. It is as if there are as many opinions as there are men.

There are times when I want to erase from my mind half the things I'm expected to learn. The overtaxed mind cannot enjoy the treasures it has obtained and it's impossible to read and fully absorb four to five books in different languages in a single day.

Before I entered Radcliffe, there was an expectation of romance, which sadly was lost. But in the transition from romantic to actual, I have learned many things which I wouldn't have if I had not felt the need to experiment. One of the most important things is learning the valuable science of patience, that teaches us that the approach towards education should be like taking a walk in the country. Our minds should be open and hospitable to anything and everything. Knowledge is power, but knowledge is also happiness, as to have true, deep knowledge is to distinguish between true and false, and between lofty and low things. Learning about thoughts and deeds that have shaped the progress of man is to experience the heartbeats of humanity through the centuries, and if one does not experience a heavenward striving in these vibrations, one must be truly deaf to the harmonies that life has to offer.

READERS' FOR BEGINNERS
THE BEST CHILDREN'S STORIES
OUR World

Chapter Nineteen

A Love Affair with Literature

Books have been so important in my education process that I shall go back to the time when I began reading. It was May 1887 when I read my first connected story. I was seven years old and from that day onwards, I have devoured every printed page that my hungry hands have felt. Initially, I had only a few books in raised print – 'Readers' for Beginners', a collection of children's stories, and a book about Earth called 'Our World'. That was all I had, I think, and I read them repeatedly, until the words were so worn out one could barely make them out. Miss Sullivan read to me sometimes, spelling

into my hand short stories and poems that she was sure I'd understand. But I liked reading myself than being read to.

I became an avid reader during my first visit to Boston. I spent a part of each day in the institution library, moving from bookcase to bookcase, looking for a book I liked. I read irrespective of whether I understood one word in ten on a page. I was fascinated by the words themselves and did not take conscious account of what I read. My mind must have been impressionable then, as I recalled many words and sentences later, even though I hadn't the faintest notion of what they meant then. Even my friends wondered at the richness of my vocabulary when I spoke these words and sentences.

When I was eight years old, my teacher discovered me reading 'The Scarlet Letter'. She gave me a book she said was better than 'Scarlet Letter' for me. It was the beautiful story of a little boy titled 'Little Lord Fauntleroy', and

she promised to read it to me the following summer. But the book was forgotten in the excitement of my seashore visit. It was only in August when Miss Sullivan narrated this story to me, and it was fascinating. Mr Anagnos had this story embossed at my request, and I read it again and again till I had it memorised. 'Little Lord Fauntleroy' was the book that truly interested me in reading. I read many books during the next two years like 'Lamb's Tales from Shakespeare', 'The Arabian Nights', 'Little Women', 'The Swiss Family Robinson', 'Heidi' and many more. I love 'The Jungle Book' and 'Wild Animals I have Known' because I love animals. I also fell in love with ancient Greece, thanks to the 'Iliad'. The Bible is also close to my heart, and reading it always gives me a sense of comfort. What can be said about Shakespeare? 'Macbeth' impressed me the most, and I read 'King Lear' and 'The Merchant of Venice' soon after. I must have been introduced to Shylock and Satan at the same time and could not help

sympathising with them. I felt no one gave them a fair chance despite their sins. They were just broken spokes in the great wheel of good, which in due course would be made whole again. I also love poetry and history, and I have read every historical work that I could get my hands on. It all began when I was gifted Swinton's 'World History' on my 13th birthday. I was introduced to French and German literature in college. The German puts strength before beauty, and truth before convention in both life and literature. The best part I like about German literature is a woman's self-sacrificing love. It is wonderfully expressed in Goethe's 'Faust'. Moliere and Racine are my favourite French writers. I also like Balzac and admire Victor Hugo. I am sorry if I have written too much about my book-friends, but that explains why my circle of friends is so limited. I like Carlyle, Wordsworth, Mark Twain and Scott too. The list, as they say is endless! In a word, literature is my Utopia.

Chapter Twenty

Other Pleasures

Reading is not my only pleasure, however, I have many other varied pleasures and amusements. I love the country and outdoor sports. I learned rowing and swimming as a little girl, and in the summertime, whenever I'm at Wrentham, Massachusetts, I practically live in my boat. I love taking my friends out rowing whenever they visit me, although I need someone to manage the rudder while I row.

Canoeing is also something I love, especially on moonlit nights. I suppose that'll make you smile knowing I cannot see the moon. But I know she's there as her luminous warmth seems

to engulf me. But my favourite amusement is sailing, and Miss Sullivan and I have had glorious sails together to McNabb's Island, Bedford Basin and York Redoubt. Even the memories are joyous!

I also have many tree friends in Wrentham. A splendid oak is one of them. Tree lore says that this king-tree stands for 800 or a 1000 years. A tradition says that under this tree the heroic Indian chief, King Philip, gazed his last on earth and sky. Another tree friend that is gentler and more approachable was a linden in the dooryard at Red Farm. A terrible thunderstorm uprooted it one day, and it broke my heart. My dog accompanies me for a walk, sail or ride whenever possible. I have had many dog-friends too - woodles, wise setters, homely bull-terriers, huge mastiffs, and soft-eyed spaniels.

I amuse myself by knitting and crocheting when a rainy day forces me to stay indoors. I also like playing a game of checkers or chess with a friend, using a special board to play. The squares are cut out, so the men stand firmly on them. The white checkers are curved on top and the black checkers are flat. The chessmen come in two sizes, with the black smaller than the white, so that people like us have no difficulty manoeuvring the pieces. I love playing solitaire when I am alone. I use playing cards marked with braille symbols in the upper right-hand corner, indicating the value of the card.

I love playing with children, and I'm happy to say that they like my company too. Going to museums, art stores and the theatre are other pleasures that I love indulging in. I recall the first time I attended the theatre 12 years ago. The little actress, Elsie Leslie was performing in the play 'The Prince and the Pauper' in Boston. It was a beautiful play, and I was allowed to go backstage and meet Elsie in her royal costume after it was over. It was a wonderful experience!

There are times though, when a sense of loneliness engulfs me like a cold mist.

Thankfully, hope arrives with a smile to whisper, "There is joy in self-forgetfulness".

So, I try and make the light in other eyes my sun, the music in other ears my symphony, and the smile on other lips my joy!

Chapter Twenty-One

Acknowledgements

If only I could enhance this sketch with the names who shaped my happiness! Some of them are famous names in literature and dear to many, while others may be totally unknown to my readers. But their influence on the lives of others shall be immortal even if they escape fame themselves. When such friends are near us, all is well. I have interacted with many men of genius. Bishop Brooks was one such man, and as a child I loved sitting on his knee, grabbing his great hand with mine. As he spoke his beautiful sermons about God, Miss Sullivan spelled them into my other hand, as I listened in delight and wonder.

"There is only one universal religion, Helen," he once replied to my puzzling query about the world having so many religions. "That is the religion of love!"

After Bishop Brooks died, I read the Bible as well as some philosophical works on religion like 'Ascent of Man' by Mr Henry Drummond. I knew the author, and his warm companionship and knowledge is a memory to cherish. I recall meeting Dr Oliver Wendell Holmes, who had invited me and Miss Sullivan to call on him. He had a lovely library and was a great human being as well as a great poet. He made me recite my favourite poem, and I visited him many times after that. We also visited the poet Whittier one summer, and he won me over with his manner and speech. I had read a book of his poems in raised print, and he was delighted when I recited a few of his poems. We became great friends, and I promised to visit him again the next summer. Tragically, he passed away before I could fulfil my promise.

Dr Edward Everett Hale is one of my oldest friends, and my love for him has only increased over the years. Ever since I was eight years old, he has supported me and Miss Sullivan in our fight. God bless him!

I have delighted in the company of Dr Alexander Graham Bell and have spent many happy days in his august company. I have had the pleasure of listening to him speak about his experiments and helped him fly kites in a way that he expects to find laws that shall determine the future air-ship. Not only is the great man an expert in many scientific fields but can also make every subject sound interesting. He has a side that is poetic and humorous as well and is happiest when he is with children. His labours for deaf children will live on forever, blessing generations of children yet to arrive in this world.

In New York, I have had the pleasure to speak with distinguished men whose names I had often heard but had never expected to meet them personally. I met most of them in the house of a good friend called

Mr Laurence Hutton. It was a pleasure visiting his lovely home, and Mrs Hutton was a true friend, and I relied on her advice to progress through college. Her letters of encouragement have lifted my spirits on difficult days. Mr Hutton introduced me to many of his literary friends, including greats like Mark Twain and William Dean Howells. I read a couple of Mark Twain's stories from his lips and felt the twinkle of his eye in his handshake.

I must mention two other friends, firstly Mrs William Thaw, of Pittsburgh who has been extremely generous to me and my teacher. I cannot mention the name of the second friend, as he likes doing good silently. He is a powerful and respectable man, and his kindness and generosity enabled me to attend college. He guided me just as he guides vast enterprises. This is how my friends have shaped the story of my life. In countless ways they have transformed my limitations into wonderful privileges and have helped me to walk proudly and happily in the shadow cast by my deprivation.

About the Author

■ Helen Adams Keller (1880–1968)

Helen Adams Keller (27 June 1880–1 June 1968) was an American author, lecturer and political activist. She has earned the distinction of being the first deaf-blind person to achieve a Bachelor of Arts degree. Helen Keller was born healthy, but an illness she contracted when she was nineteen months old left her both deaf and blind.

Helen Keller is the author of 12 published books and many articles. When she was just 22 years old, Helen Keller published her autobiography, 'The Story of My Life', in 1903. She was aided in this effort by her governess and friend, Anne Sullivan and Sullivan's husband, John Macy. Helen Keller wrote her autobiography while she was in college and this account features her insights about the world. Keller devoted much of her later life to raising funds for the American Foundation for the Blind. She breathed her last in her sleep on 1 June 1968, just a few weeks short of her eighty-eighth birthday.

■ List of Main Characters

Helen Keller: The protagonist and the author of this memoir, Helen Keller was left both deaf and blind early at an early age. With the help of her teacher, Anne Sullivan, she battled and overcame all obstacles to emerge as the first deaf-blind person to obtain a bachelor's degree.

Anne Sullivan: Anne Sullivan was blind in her youth and decided to dedicate her life to teaching the blind after her vision was partially restored. Her tenacity, patience, and skill helped Helen reach great heights, something that was totally unexpected.

Kate Adams: Helen and Mildred's mother, Kate Adams, was a caring woman who taught Helen many things. She supported her and loved her throughout her life.

Arthur H. Keller: Helen and Mildred's father, Arthur H. Keller was a captain in the Confederate Army before he became a newspaper editor. Helen was devastated by his death in 1896.

Mildred Keller: Mildred is the younger sister of Helen Keller. Helen was jealous of her sister for a long time, but the two sisters became close slowly and shared an inseparable bond.

Mr Anagnos: Michael Anagnos was the Director of Perkins Institute for the Blind, and a good friend of Helen's. But his relationship with Helen became strained because of a short story unknowingly plagiarised by Helen.

Dr Alexander Graham Bell: The inventor of the telephone, Helen's friend and a teacher of the deaf; Helen dedicated her autobiography to the great man, who spent a lot of time with her.

■ Questions

Chapter 1

- 1. *Briefly describe what Helen has to say about her ancestors.*
- 2. *How did Helen lose her sight and hearing?*

Chapter 2

- 1. *Who were Helen's best friends?*
- 2. *Who was Martha? What did Helen and Martha do together?*

Chapter 3

- 1. *Where was Helen going and why?*
- 2. *Who made the doll for Helen? Why didn't Helen like the doll?*

Chapter 4

- 1. *How did Helen come to know that something unusual was about to happen at home?*
- 2. *How did Helen learn her first word?*

Chapter 5

- 1. *Why didn't Helen climb a tree for a long time?*
- 2. *What was the tree of paradise and how did it influence Helen?*

Chapter 6

- 1. *Why did Helen ask few questions when her teacher introduced her to a new thing?*
- 2. *How did Miss Sullivan explain the meaning of 'love' to Helen?*

Chapter 7

- 1. *What method was used by Miss Sullivan to teach Helen how to read?*
- 2. *Describe the incident with the tadpoles.*

Chapter 8

- *1. Why did Helen look forward to the Christmas season?*
- *2. What surprise did Helen and Miss Sullivan have for the others?*

Chapter 9

- *1. Why did Helen go to Boston?*
- *2. Who was Nancy? What was the problem with her?*

Chapter 10

- *1. Where did Helen read about the ocean?*
- *2. Describe Helen's encounter with the ocean.*

Chapter 11

- *1. What was Fern Quarry? Describe the place in detail.*
- *2. Who was Black Beauty? Why had she been named so?*

Chapter 12

- *1. What was Helen's favourite pastime in winter? How did she go about it?*
- *2. Who was Miss Fuller? How did she teach Helen how to speak?*

Chapter 13

- *1. What was 'Frost King' and who wrote it?*
- *2. What was Mr Anagnos's initial reaction after reading the story? Why was he embarrassed later?*

Chapter 14

- *1. Why did Helen experience a strange fear when she tried to write something?*
- *2. Describe the progress that Helen made in her studies.*

Chapter 15

- *1. How did Helen progress at the Wright Humason school?*

- 2. *Why was Helen disappointed with this school later?*

Chapter 16

- 1. *Describe Helen's initial experiences at Cambridge.*
- 2. *What type of special books were prepared for Helen here?*

Chapter 17

- 1. *What were the problems Helen encountered in her second year at Gilman School?*
- 2. *What methods did Helen apply to learn geometry and physics?*

Chapter 18

- 1. *Who taught math to Helen? Why was it decided to have another year of tuition?*
- 2. *Why was Helen unable to take notes in class? How did she deal with the problem?*

Chapter 19

- 1. *Which book made Helen an avid reader? Describe how it happened.*
- 2. *What were Helen's views about Shakespeare?*

Chapter 20

- 1. *What were Helen's favourite activities other than reading?*
- 2. *Who were Helen's unique friends and how did she feel in their company?*

Chapter 21

- 1. *Who taught Helen about the religion of love and how?*
- 2. *Who were Helen's celebrity friends? How did Helen meet these people?*